A New Paradigm for the Iraqi Police: Applying Community-Oriented Policing to Iraqi Police Development

A Monograph

by

Major Florentino Santana
United States Army

MENS EST CLAVIS VICTORIAE

School of Advanced Military Studies
United States Army Command and General Staff College
Fort Leavenworth, Kansas

AY 2008

REPORT DOCUMENTATION PAGE

Form Approved
OMB No. 0704-0188

1. REPORT DATE *(DD-MM-YYYY)*	2. REPORT TYPE	3. DATES COVERED *(From - To)*
30-040-2009	Monograph	July 2008-May 2009

4. TITLE AND SUBTITLE	5a. CONTRACT NUMBER
A new Paradigm for Iraqi Police: Applying Community-Oriented Policing to Iraqi Police Training	
	5b. GRANT NUMBER
	5c. PROGRAM ELEMENT NUMBER

6. AUTHOR(S)	5d. PROJECT NUMBER
Major Florentino Santana	
	5e. TASK NUMBER
	5f. WORK UNIT NUMBER

7. PERFORMING ORGANIZATION NAME(S) AND ADDRESS(ES)	8. PERFORMING ORGANIZATION REPORT NUMBER
Advanced Military Studies Program 250 Gibbon Ave Fort Leavenworth,KS 66027-213	

9. SPONSORING / MONITORING AGENCY NAME(S) AND ADDRESS(ES)	10. SPONSOR/MONITOR'S ACRONYM(S)
Command and General Staff College 1 Reynolds Ave Fort Leavenworth, KS 66027	CGSC, SAMS
	11. SPONSOR/MONITOR'S REPORT NUMBER(S)

12. DISTRIBUTION / AVAILABILITY STATEMENT

Approved for Public Release

13. SUPPLEMENTARY NOTES

14. ABSTRACT

Policing can be an effective counterinsurgency tool. Police are able to determine the individual needs of each community and address each constituency's concern which in turn enhances the government's legitimacy. The Iraqi Police face the challenge of transforming themselves from an institution that served the state to an institution that serves the people. They have so far failed to achieve that paradigm shift. Commanders in the field that have recently executed the Police Transition mission, as well as experts in the Iraqi Police training process, admit that after years and millions of dollars in training and equipping, their developmental progress lags behind that of the military. Iraqi Police, however, have models of behavior they can rely on that are compatible with this change. Introducing the Community-Oriented Policing (COP) philosophy into their training may provide a reliable model of behavior to help the Iraqi Police accomplish this transformation. Their ability to change may have a direct impact on the legitimacy and success of the Government of Iraq (GOI). The success of the GOI may directly impact the United State's National Strategic Objectives.

15. SUBJECT TERMS

Iraqi Police,Counterinsurgency,COIN,Community-Oriented Policing,COP,Strategic-Orieted Policing,SOP,Neighborhood-Oriented Polincing,NOP, Problem-Oriented Policing,POP,Social Control,Crime Prevention

16. SECURITY CLASSIFICATION OF:			17. LIMITATION OF ABSTRACT	18. NUMBER OF PAGES	19a. NAME OF RESPONSIBLE PERSON Stefan J. Banach,COL ,U.S. Army
a. REPORT UNCLASSIFIED	b. ABSTRACT UNCLASSIFIED	c. THIS PAGE UNCLASSIFIED	UNLIMITED	54	19b. TELEPHONE NUMBER *(include area code)* 913-758-3302

Standard Form 298 (Rev. 8-98)
Prescribed by ANSI Std. Z39.18

SCHOOL OF ADVANCED MILITARY STUDIES

MONOGRAPH APPROVAL

Major Florentino Santana

Title of Monograph: A New Paradigm for the Iraqi Police: Applying Community-Oriented Policing to Iraqi Police Development

This monograph was defended by the degree candidate on 9 April 2009 and approved by the monograph director and reader named below.

Approved by:

_____   Monograph Director
Lester W. Grau

_____   Seminar Leader
Jeffrey Goble, COL, SF

_____   Monograph Reader
Jacob Kipp, PhD

_____   Monograph Reader
Douglas Overdeer

_____   Director,
Stefan J. Banach, COL, IN   School of Advanced
                                             Military Studies

_____   Director,
Robert F. Baumann, Ph.D.   Graduate Degree
                                             Programs

Abstract

A NEW PARADIGM FOR THE IRAQI POLICE: APPLYING COMMUNITY-ORIENTED POLICING TO IRAQI POLICE DEVELOPMENT by MAJ Florentino Santana, USA, 54 pages.

Policing can be an effective counterinsurgency tool. Police are able to determine the individual needs of each community and address each constituency's concern which in turn enhances the government's legitimacy. The Iraqi Police face the challenge of transforming themselves from an institution that served the state to an institution that serves the people. They have so far failed to achieve that paradigm shift. Commanders in the field that have recently executed the Police Transition mission, as well as experts in the Iraqi Police training process, admit that after years and millions of dollars in training and equipping, their developmental progress lags behind that of the military. They attribute the difference in progress to corrupt practices left over from Saddam Hussein's regime, sectarian loyalty, militia infiltration, and lack of experienced leadership. Few Iraqi Police, however, have models of behavior they can rely on that are compatible with this paradigm shift. Introducing the Community-Oriented Policing (COP) philosophy into their training may provide a reliable model of behavior to help the Iraqi Police accomplish this. Their ability to change may have a direct impact on the legitimacy and success of the Government of Iraq (GOI). The success of the GOI may directly impact the United State's National Strategic Objectives.

COP is a philosophy with new paradigm. It is a philosophy that provides a complete cohesive organizational plan for modifying police work to achieve effective crime prevention. COP is a philosophy, not a program. It requires the police and the community to cooperate in identifying problems, then work together to solve them. In order for the COP to work, everyone in the police organization must commit to the philosophy. Police officers have to motivate the community to participate in police auxiliary activities. Decentralization and flatter organizations are a necessity. Institutions cannot create a specialized COP unit. The institution has to change.

The monograph first lays out how COP is compatible with COIN theories and doctrine. The monograph explores the evolution of policing as a means of social control and crime prevention in Western societies. The COP philosophy emerged as an effective crime prevention methodology. The monograph defines COP and explains its different components. It explores non Western experiences with social control and crime prevention as micro-histories in India, Nigeria, and Israel. A comparison model displays common social control mechanisms within all three countries. The monograph also addresses how time has played a factor in the evolution of crime prevention and the adoption of COP to balance the crime prevention responsibilities between the government and communities in India, Nigeria, and Israel. It also discusses conditions that prevented a similar evolution in Iraq. The monograph closes with a conclusion applicable to the situation in Iraq and offers recommendations for COP implementation.

TABLE OF CONTENTS

Introduction

The Iraqi Police face the challenge of transforming themselves from an institution that served the state to an institution that serves the people. They have so far failed to achieve this. Commanders in the field that have recently executed the Police Transition mission, as well as experts in the Iraqi Police training process, admit that after years and millions of dollars in training and equipping, their developmental progress lags behind that of the military. They attribute the difference in progress to corrupt practices left over from Saddam Hussein's regime, sectarian loyalty, militia infiltration, and lack of experienced leadership. "Few Iraqi Police, however, have models of behavior they can rely on that are compatible with this paradigm shift."[1]

The police are the most visible government institution in counterinsurgency (COIN) operations. William Rosenau stated that, "it is no doubt true that in internal conflict environment, the civilian police, relative to the army or national intelligence services, are likely to have more access to civilian population."[2] David Galula stated, "the eye and arm of the government in all matters pertaining to internal order, the police are a key factor...."[3] Field Manual (FM) 3-24 *Counterinsurgency* states, "The primary frontline COIN force is often the police not the military. The primary COIN objective is to enable local institutions. Therefore, supporting the police is essential."[4]

Police training is essential to victory in Iraq and victory in Iraq is essential to the accomplishment of U. S. strategic objectives. The 2005 National Strategy for Victory in Iraq defines Iraq as the central front on the global war on terror. It establishes success in Iraq as being essential in the long war against international terrorism. It stated that victory in Iraq will be in

---

[1] Tony Pfaff, *Development and Reform of the Iraqi Police Forces,* Carlisle: United States Army War College, 2006, 7.

[2] William Rosenau, Low-Cost Trigger Pullers: The Politics of Policing in the Context of State Building and Counterinsurgency. Washington D.C. : RAND National Security Research Division, 2008, 7.

[3] David Galula. *Counterinsurgency Warfare: Theory and Practice,* St. Petersburg: Hailer Publishing, 2005, 31. In this section, Galula is speaking on the side of the insurgent, however, the converse is still relevant to COIN.

[4] Headquarters Department of the Army. *Field Manual 3-24 Counterinsurgency,* Washington D.C., December 2006, page 6-19, paragraph 6-90

stages and defined these stages as short term, medium term and longer term. In the short term coalition forces need the development of a strong security forces that make steady progress in fighting terrorism and neutralizing the insurgency. In the medium term Iraqi security forces lead the way in defeating terrorists and insurgents. In the long term Iraqi security forces defeat the terrorists and insurgents while upholding the rule of law. A competent Iraqi Police force is critical to these objectives. The same document establishes security as one of the "tracks" in the strategy for victory in Iraq. The objective is to develop the Iraqi capabilities to secure their own country while they defeat terrorist and insurgents. They clear areas of enemy control by capturing or killing fighters while denying them safe-haven. Then security forces hold the areas by ensuring that they remain under government control. The March 2006 National Security Strategy (NSS) reiterates these objectives. In the President's opening letter he stated, "…we are fighting alongside Iraqis to secure a united, stable, and democratic Iraq - a new ally in the war on terror in the heart of the Middle East."[5]

Introducing the Community-Oriented Policing (COP) philosophy into their training would provide a reliable model of behavior to help the Iraqi Police accomplish this. Their ability to change may have a direct impact on the legitimacy and success of the Government of Iraq (GOI). The success of the GOI directly impacts of the United State's National Strategic Objectives.

Methodology
The monograph first explores the evolution of policing as a means of social control and crime prevention in Western societies. It also explores how the relationship between the police and the community evolved as police became efficient professional entities looking for more effective crime prevention methods. The COP philosophy emerged as an effective crime

---

[5] Executive Officer of the President of the United States. *The National Security Strategy of the United States of America.* Washigton D.C., 2006, The President's introductory letter..

2

prevention methodology. The monograph defines COP and explains its different components. It also lays out how it is compatible with COIN theories and doctrine.

The monograph explores non Western experiences with social control and crime prevention as micro-histories in India, Nigeria, and Israel. The research focuses on each country's social control and crime prevention traditions prior to their colonial periods, during colonial rule, and after achieving independence. It also looks at their experience with COP. The monograph then applies to research on Iraq. The monograph compares the four countries to determine commonalities in their social control traditions that would influence their experiences with COP and crime prevention.

A comparison model displays common social control mechanisms within all three countries. The monograph also addresses how time has played a factor in the evolution of crime prevention and the adoption of COP to balance the crime prevention responsibilities between the government and communities in India, Nigeria, and Israel. It also discusses conditions that prevented a similar evolution in Iraq. The monograph closes with a conclusion applicable to the situation in Iraq and offers recommendations.

Policing and Counterinsurgency Operations

Policing can be an effective counterinsurgency tool. COP is a philosophy that establishes the community as its center of gravity (COG) in the fight against crime. FM 3-24 agrees that police are the most visible institution of the government's response to an insurgency. Different interests. Police are able to determine the individual needs of each community to address each constituency's concern which in turn enhances the government's legitimacy. Community Oriented Policing is compatible with the Clear, Hold, Build strategy established in the 2005 National Strategy for Victory in Iraq.

COP is a mindset. Crime fighting efforts revolve around the citizen. Military officers can extract a useful analogy from David Galula who proposes that the population is the objective in a counterinsurgency and stated, "if the insurgent manages to dissociate the population from the counterinsurgent, to control it physically, to get its active support, he will win the war because, in the final analysis, the exercise of political power depends on the tacit or explicit agreement of the population or, at worst, on its submissiveness."[6]

The primary COIN objective is to support local institutions; therefore, supporting the police is essential."[7] In COP the police are instrumental in supporting the community, at the most local level possible, to identify problems. The police then are advocates for the community in addressing those problems regardless of whether or not the problem is a criminal matter. In essence, the police become the conduit by which other government agencies address quality of life issues in the community. The COP philosophy then helps COIN operations not only in the security line, but in terms of all Logical Lines of Operations (LLO)[8]. Police provide civil security, while assisting in the delivery of essential services, as determined by the community. This leads

---

[6]David Galula, *Counterinsurgency Warfare*, 7.

[7] Headquarters Department of the Army, *Field Manual 3-24. Counterinsurgency*, page 6-19, paragraph 6-90

[8] "Commanders use LLOs to visualize, describe, and direct operations against enemies that hide among the populance. A plan based on LLO unifies the efforts of joint, interagency, multinational, and HN forces toward a common purpose." Headquarters Department of the Army. "Field Manual 3-24." *Counterinsurgency*. Washington D.C., December 2006, page 5-3, paragraph 5-7.

to the legitimacy of government and economic development, assisted by information operations. This maintains the community in constant contact with police, and therefore, the government.

Legitimacy of the government is critical in counterinsurgency. United States Army Field Manual 3-24 *Counterinsurgency states,* "Success in counterinsurgency (COIN) operations requires establishing a legitimate government supported by the people and able to address the fundamental causes that insurgents use to gain support."[9] Bard O'Neill asks the question, "…is the government attuned to the fact that normally the elite and the masses have different interests and respond to different insurgent appeals, thus raising the possibility of the government's adopting policies tailored to each and driving a wedge between the two?"[10] The underlying idea is that different parts of the population have different interests and the government's legitimacy depends on how well they address the particular interests of each constituency. COP established the premise that each community has different problems and concerns; thus placing the community in a position to determine the priorities.

Clear, Hold, Build

Community Oriented Policing is compatible with the clear, hold, and build strategy. The 2005 National Strategy for Victory in Iraq established the United States efforts along three tracks: a political track, security track, and an economic track. An effective police force was part of the security track, with the stated objective of developing the Iraqi's capability to secure their country, carry out a campaign to defeat terrorism, and neutralize the insurgents. United Stated forces in Iraq would assist Iraqi Security Forces (ISF) to "*clear* areas of enemy control by remaining on the offensive, killing and capturing enemy fighters and denying them safe-haven. *Hold* areas freed from enemy control by ensuring that they remain under the control of a peaceful

---

[9] Headquarters Department of the Army, *Field M 3-24 Counterinsurgency,* page 6-1, paragraph 6-1.

[10] Bard E. O'Neill. Insurgency *& Terrorism: From Revolution to Apocalypse 2nd ed.* Dulles: Potomac Books, 2005. 169.

Iraqi government with adequate ISF presence. *Build* ISF and the capacity of local institutions to deliver services, advance the rule of law, and nurture civil society."[11]

The explanation of how COP actually works is covered in the next chapter; nevertheless, the police use Strategic-Oriented Policing (SOP) to surge traditional methods such as directed patrols, aggressive patrols, and saturation patrols to *clear* criminals from an area. The police must *hold* the effort for some time to allow the community to *build* the mechanisms and programs that will prevent the return of the particular criminal activity. The remaining components (Neighborhood-Oriented Policing and Problem-Oriented Policing) are a continuation of the *build* phase, as the communities establish mechanisms to identify, prioritize, and solve quality of life issues in conjunction with police whether or not the problems are criminal in nature.

Gary D. Calese draws a parallel between organized crime, criminal youth gangs, and insurgents based on several structural factors: leadership, organization, culture, and finances. He compares the criminal organizations to insurgents to make the overarching argument that, "the law enforcement community has a wealth of knowledge about Mafia style organized crime, youth gangs, and criminal behavior in general."[12] He advocates for law enforcement methods can be useful in COIN. Among the methods he mentions are capture-over-kill mentality, identification verification, intelligence software, street knowledge, and COP. Calese likens COP to John J. McCuen's oil spot strategy in which police and military provide safe zones for themselves and the population in a particular community. "The police and other government forces gain legitimacy by proving they can protect the citizens...Those people, in turn, feel safe enough to work with the government and against the insurgents."[13]

Simply creating police or stating that COP is a philosophy does little to implement it as a tool in a COIN situation. In order to understand its usefulness and incorporate it into planning

---

[11] National Security Council. *The National Strategy for Victory in Iraq.* Washigton D.C., 2005, 8.
[12] Gary D. Calese, *Law Enforcement Methods for Counterinsurgency Operations,* Fort Leavenworth: School of Advanced Military Studies, 2005, 46.
[13] Ibid,43.

one must understand its origins and its design. This is not a new philosophy; COP is the product of years of police doctrine (common practices) and COP continues to evolve. Use as a tool in COIN is another part of its evolution.

Development of Policing

Policing is defined as "people authorized by a group of people to regulate interpersonal relations within groups through the application of physical forces." [14] It is a function that emerges from the community's need to enforce social control norms and prevent crime. Social control theorist Travis Hirschi explains that, "the attachments to our peers, schools, parents, and spouses all keep us from committing criminal behavior." [15]

The relationship between those chosen to enforce the norms and the community has evolved. Robert Friedman models five different possible relationships between the police and the community. The first relationship is one in which they are mutually exclusive. This is very rare. The police are recruited from the community. When they are not at work, they live in the community. The second possible relationship is when they completely overlap. In this relationship, the police and the community are one and the same. According to Friedman, this only occurs in a police academy situation where the academy class represents that particular community. He invalidates this as a logical option because the scenario is very particular, rare, and short in duration. The third relationship is the police encompasses the community. This happens in a police state where everyone collects information on everyone else for the police. In the fourth relationship, the community is all encompassing of the police. The community has internal social control forces that allow it to police itself. Friedman uses the Amish communities as an example. "Deviance and rule infractions occur in these communities but they are always or mostly self-contained, and are either tolerated quietly or punished in the extreme, sometimes by ostracization or even deportation of the violator." In the fifth relationship, the community and

---

[14] Steven P. Lab, and Dilip K Das. *International Perspective on Community Policing and Crime Prevention*: Upper Saddle River, New Jersey: Prentice Hall 2003, 227 Dilip quotes Byley in 1987.

[15] Willard M. Oliver, *Community-Oriented Policing: A Systematic Approach to Policing*, New Jersey: Prentice Hall, 1998, 93.

police partially overlap. The community establishes a law enforcement that deals with all the criminals according to the rules the community establishes. [16]

the code of Hammurabi is the first record written laws and punishment dating back to 2100 B.C. It was written in ancient Babylon, located in modern day Iraq. The military conducted early law enforcement and that changed little for centuries. The first efforts at organizing civilian law enforcement were in the British Isles during the 9th Century. Anglo-Saxon King Alfred mandated the Frank Pledge. It was the first system of policing that integrated members of the community into policing the community. That system remained in place until the Norman invasion in the 11th Century when law enforcement functions again became a responsibility of the military. King John's signature on the Magna-Carta in 1215 granted certain rights to the people, which cleared the way for the 1285 Statute of Winchester. The statute revised successful policing practices. All males 15 to 60 years of age were required to maintain weapons at their residences and participate in day and night patrols. This system remained the model for approximately 500 years. [17]

Rising crime during the Industrial Revolution in 18th Century England led merchant and magistrate Patrick Colquhoun to propose the establishment of a metropolitan police force in 1789. The citizenry rejected the idea but Colquhoun planted the seed in their social conscience. In 1829 Sir Robert Peel, as Home Secretary, used Colquhoun's idea to establish the first formal police department in England. Sir Robert Peel established twelve principles that became the fundamentals for police departments in the western world. Peel's Principles were:

> *1. The police must be stable, efficient, and organized along military lines.*
> *2. The police must be under government control.*
> *3. The absence of crime will best prove the efficiency of police.*
> *4. The distribution of crime news is essential.*
> *5. Proper deployment of police strength, by both time and area, is essential.*

---

[16] Robert R. Friedman, *Community Policing: Comparative Perspective and Prospects*: New York: St. Martin's Press, 1992, 14-16, This paragraph explains Freidman's concept of the possible relationships between police and the community. Friedman's quote included in the paragraph came from page 16.
[17] Willard M. Oliver, *Community-Oriented Policing*, 1998, 3-4.

9

6. No quality is more indispensable to a policeman than a perfect command of temper. A quiet, determined manner has more effect than violent action.
7. Good appearance commands respect.
8. The selection and training of proper persons are at the root of efficient law enforcement.
9. Public security demands that every police officer be given an identifying number.
10. Police headquarters should be centrally located and easily accessible to people.
11. Policemen should be hired on a probationary basis before permanent assignment.
12. Police crime records are necessary for the best distribution of police strength.[18]

Police development in the United States followed the same basic traditions as England. Between the establishment of the first settlement in Jamestown, Virginia and the Declaration of Independence, law enforcement was in the hand of a sheriff. In 1776, the values promulgated in the Declaration of Independence established a new relationship between the people and their government. The declaration states, "We hold these truths to be self-evident, that all men are created equal, that they are endowed by their Creator with certain unalienable Rights, that among these are Life, Liberty and the pursuit of Happiness. — that to secure these rights, Governments are instituted among Men, deriving their just powers from the consent of the governed,"[19] This established the government's responsibility to protect the people, and further, that government is the people. The Founding Fathers wrote the United States Constitution based on the principles listed above. Oliver uses the preamble to establish his argument on the role of the police. The preamble of the Constitution states, "We the people of the United States, in Order to form a more perfect Union, establish *Justice, insure domestic Tranquility*, provide for the common defence, promote the general *Welfare*, and secure the Blessings of Liberty to ourselves and our Posterity, do ordain and establish this Constitution for the United States of America."[20] Oliver's argument is that the police are the government's instrument to ensure justice is served, to maintain order, and therefore insure domestic tranquility. Oliver also argues that law and order services promote the general welfare of the people. Oliver states, "the ability for people to live without fear in their

---

[18] Willard M. Oliver, *Community-Oriented Policing:*, 4-5. Oliver cites Sir Robert Peel's rules.
[19] *United States Declaration of Independence,* The first two sentences in the second full paragraph
[20] *United States Constitution*, preamble, The author added emphasis on words concerned with the establishment of welfare of the people, justice and tranquility (order).

communities is important to the overall health of the nation, and the Founding Father understood this important concept."[21]

The first formal United States police departments were the Boston Police Department (1838), the New York Police Department (1845), and Philadelphia Police Department (1854). Police departments continued to develop in the United States throughout the 19th and 20th century. As a profession, policing went through periods of transformations. During the early days, politics determined the authority and activity of police. The profession suffered from corruption, and low respect. From the 1930s through early 1980s, policing underwent a period of professionalization and reform.[22]

Several prominent thinkers emerged. Among them are Chief August Vollmer and his protégé O.W. Wilson. Vollmer became the first Chief of Police of the Berkeley Police Department. He introduced the department to many innovations that are part of policing today. Innovations included radios in patrol cars, finger printing, hand writing analysis, the establishment of criminal databases, and the use of polygraph tests. He believed in training all police officers in criminal investigation methods.[23]

O. W. Wilson graduated from University of California at Berkley and worked for the Berkley Police Department. He was Vollmer's student. He applied Vollmer's ideas as Police Chief of Fullerton, California and Wichita, Kansas in the 1950s. He believed that police had to be honest and worked to eliminate corruption. He was known as a reformer. In 1960, he became Superintendent of Police in Chicago, Illinois. He implemented several measures to eliminate corruption and restore faith in the Department. He established a civilian review board free of political influence, established a merit-based promotion system, reinforced the disciplinary system, and moved his office to police headquarters. He also redrew precinct boundaries different

---

[21] Willard M. Oliver, *Community-Oriented Policing*, 7.
[22] Ibid, 11.
[23] University of Central Missouri. *August Vollmer.* October 2008. http://www.ucmo.edu/x74744.xml (accessed October 25, 2008)

from political boundaries. During his tenure, the department could claim better response times, higher officer morale, and a better public image.

These reforms ushered in *Traditional Policing*. In *Traditional Policing,* the police department is a highly centralized government agency with the goal of prosecuting serious violent crime. Response times are the standard by which to measure police efficiency. It measures the amount of time between the police receiving a call and an officer's arrival. Statistics measured the officer's production. Arrest rates, citations issued, and incident reports written measured officers' efficiency. The role of the police administration was to provide the necessary, rules, policies, and procedures to prevent corruption. Officers also expected administrators to work with other agencies, the media, and the community "so they can get on with the job."[24]

Traditional Policing became the accepted model but ignored the community. George Kelling stated, "police were perceived as impersonal or oriented toward crime solving rather than responsive to the emotional crisis of the victim."[25] Anyone that has ever seen an episode of the Hollywood police show "Dragnet" will remember Police Sergeant Joe Friday interviewing a distraught victim saying, "the facts …, just the facts." That was a reflection of this time.

The Founding Fathers understood that it was important for people to live in their communities without fear. *Traditional Policing's* reactive focus did nothing to affect the community's level of fear. Increasing people's positive contact with police, who focused on what was important to them, decreased their fear regardless of the actual in crime rate.[26]

Police departments worked on involving the community with a series of programs during the mid 1970s and early 1980s. These programs were based on a *Police-Community Relations* approach. Police needed to understand the diverse people it dealt with and the people needed to understand how the police operated. The Police Explorers, DARE, civilian ride-along progrorem,

---

[24] Willard M. Oliver, *Community-Oriented*, 13.
[25] Ibid, 12. Oliver sites Kelling and Moore in 1988.
[26] Friedman, Robert R, *Community Policing: Comparative Perspective and Prospects,* New York: St. Martin's Press, 1992, 45.

and community relations teams were some of those initiatives. *Police-Community Relations* as a program failed because it became just that, a program that diverted scarce police resources from the efficiency driven goals of the departments. It "required a rethinking of the social and formal organization of policing on a massive scale."[27]

In 1979, Herman Goldstein questioned the established notion of efficient policing. He argued that police departments had focused so much on the means (enforcing the law) and forgotten the ends (solving problems) of policing. Police had reached the zenith of administrative competence and were unwilling to venture beyond "toward creating a more systemic concern for the end product of their efforts."[28]

Goldstein argued that environmental pressure from city governments' would push police agencies to adopt a results oriented method to solve their communities' problems. These pressures included: 1) City government's reluctance to spend more money on police resources without a reasonable expectation of success. 2) Research questioning the effectiveness of preventive patrols and existing investigative procedures. 3) Growth of a consumer-oriented public demanding improved police services based on results. 4) Research showing that the best managed agencies that could not demonstrate better results in their communities than communities with less-developed police departments. 5) Internal resistance to organizational changes pushing police administrators to demonstrate to officers that the sacrifice of implementing new programs would be worth the effort.

He called that approach *Problem-Oriented Policing*. Implementing an overall process would require police departments to:

> *"...identify in precise terms the problem that citizens look for the police to handle. Once identified each problem must be explored in great detail. What do we know about the problem? Has it been researched? If so, with what results? What should we know? Is it a proper concern of government? What authority and resources are available for dealing with it? What is the current police response? In the broadest-ranging search*

---

[27] Willard M. Oliver, *Community-Oriented Policing*, 17. Oliver quotes Jack R. Greene in 1987.
[28] Herman Goldstein, Improving Policing: A Problem Oriented Approach." *Thinking About Police*, Edited by Carl Klockars and Stephen D. Mastrofski. New York: McGraw-Hill, 1991, 481.

13

for solutions, what would constitute the most intelligent response? What factors should be considered in choosing from among alternatives? If a new response is adopted, how does one go about evaluating its effectiveness? And finally, what changes, if any, does implementation of a more effective response require in the police organization. [29]

This type of methodology was not foreign to departments used to conducting rigorous studies of administrative problem. The difference was focusing on the problems the community thought to be important. Calls for a systematic community based approach to policing that propelled the emergence of *Community-Oriented Policing*. It was a combination of Sir Robert Peel's principles with Goldstein's problem oriented methods.

---

[29] Herman Goldstein, Improving Policing: A Problem Oriented Approach.", 483.

Community-Oriented Policing

"Community Oriented Policing (COP)… is a new paradigm. It is an orientation that provides a complete cohesive organizational plan for modifying police work to achieve effective crime prevention."[30] COP is a philosophy, not a program. It requires the police and the community to cooperate in identifying problems, then work together to solve them. In order for COP to work, everyone in the police organization must commit to the philosophy. Police officers have to motivate the community to participate in police auxiliary activities. Decentralized organizations are a necessity. Institutions cannot create a specialized COP unit. Institutions have to change

It is the police officer's task to foster a sense of community in the area that he or she works. An individual officer may intuitively take time to talk to business owners, religious leaders, and school officials in his or her area to form bonds that would help him or her deal with problems. The goal of COP is for police departments to make that type of action explicit. Oliver called this "the formalization of informal customs and the routinization of spontaneous events."[31] Police place a high level of importance on contact with the individual citizen. That leads to increased interaction between the police and citizens which develops a sense of community spirit. This gives officers the opportunity to become aware of the community's concerns.

When police and the community come together, they identify and prioritize problems that are specific to the particular community and set goals for possible solutions. This combined effort produces cooperation in the search for possible solutions. Both police and the community work on developing programs that will help implement the possible solutions that fall within local legal boundaries. Implementation of the programs result in a series of expected police operational practices to make the programs work. Oliver offers examples of some programs when he stated,

---

[30] Steven P Lab. and Dilip K. Das. *International Perspective on Community Policing and Crime Prevention*, 224, quoting Oliver and Bartgis in 1998.
[31] Willard M. Oliver, *Community-Oriented Policing*, 34.

"the programs could include: community meetings, neighborhood watch, bike patrol, police youth league, and police mini-stations in the community...."[32]

To operationalize the underlying theme in COP, "...the police and the community working together creating solutions to the indigenous problems that plague their community, and implementing programs to solve these problems."[33] Oliver describes three important components: Strategic-Oriented Policing (SOP), Neighborhood-Oriented Policing (NOP), and Problem-Oriented Policing (POP).

SOP expands the procedures and practices of traditional policing that will enable the implementation of all aspects of COP. Slightly modifying existing police procedures gives officers and the community time to slowly adapt to the new philosophy. These existing police procedures are directed patrol, aggressive patrol, or saturation patrol tactics focused on high crime areas. Resource shortages prevent most departments from surging in specific areas for an extended period of time; something else has to replace that physical police presence. The purpose is to displace criminals and let the community establish programs that will prevent the return of the particular criminal activity. This is where the transition to NOP occurs.

The first step in SOP is to identify geographic areas to focus police efforts. The department must use existing criminal information and information provided through dialog with officers who know where the community thinks it needs the additional police presence. The old way of measuring effectiveness by expecting that higher arrest rates will yield a lower crime rate has to change. Quality of life in the community underlies effective law enforcement. Quality of live can express itself as a reduction in fear and a more positive perspective of the level of crime in the community.

Directed patrol is the easiest action to implement. Determining the location that will receive the extra patrol can be done through the officer's discretion, crime analysis, and

---

[32] Willard M. Oliver, *Community-Oriented Policing*, 38.
[33] Ibid, 48.

community complaints. The shift supervisor at a particular police precinct can take extra patrol officers in the shift and place them under one of the shift sergeants. This *ad hoc* unit can focus on locations needing attention throughout the precinct.

Aggressive patrol means an increase in police contact with offenders in a specific area. A police officer working a high drug area can use field interview stops, traffic enforcement, sting operations, as well as littering and loud music ordinances to both disrupt the drug dealers and reduce the traffic of drug buyers in specific locations.

Saturation patrol is the most resource intensive because it requires the gathering of officers from throughout the department to saturate an area. A department can pull a few officers out of their usual patrol duties and form at team that can vary its shift hours and days off to flood needed areas for an extended period of time. The purpose is to displace the targeted criminal activity.

NOP requires the existence of a neighborhood committee as the conduit of information and concerns. If the community does not have a system to communicate and address concerns, the police must take the initiative in establishing support for the formation of such committees. In the communities that have an established system, the police must integrate into the existing system. Once the conduit of information is working, it becomes possible to identify problems and implement solutions according to the community's goals.

NOP can be considered the second phase of implementation; it is the heart of COP and can happen simultaneously with SOP. For it to work, the community cannot be seen as an ally or as just a partner in the fight against crime. It has to be at the head of the organization to which police are responsible and accountable. Oliver gives several examples of NOP programs: community patrols, community crime prevention, communication programs, and community social control programs.[34]

---

[34] Willard M. Oliver, *Community-Oriented Policing*, 81.

Community patrols are the assignment of patrol officers to specific communities that enable departments to establish a strong police presence in the chosen area. These officers are a visible and accessible part of the community. The most used examples of these programs are the implementation of walking patrols and bicycle patrols.

Community crime prevention encompasses some programs that have been in existence since the 1960s and the Police-Community Relations days. The focus of crime prevention programs are to team up with business, churches, and community residents to identify possible targets of criminal activity and take preventive action. The programs can include business and residential security surveys, Neighborhood Watch, and Drug Abuse Resistance Education (DARE).

Communication programs are those designed to open lines of communication between police and the community. The purpose of this program is to show the community who the police officers are and how they operate. Community members learn why police take certain actions and, utilize various procedures, and how can citizens assist. Among the initiatives police departments use include Citizen Ride-Along Programs, where citizens get to ride with an on duty patrol officer for a shift, and Citizen Police Academies, where citizens attend a short training session that gives them a flavor of how police officers train.

Community social control programs are based on social control theory. The purpose of this program is to team up with the community in supporting initiatives that will strengthen personal bonds. Lions Club Law Camp, Fraternal Order of Police Summer Camp, and Career Camp are example of such initiatives.

POP is Herman Goldstein's concept of efficiency and effectiveness discussed earlier in this monograph. "Problem-Oriented Policing addresses a particular problem, analyses the problem, determines a course of action, implements the program, then follows up in an evaluative manner. If the problem is resolved, the police and community must only keep the problem in check. If it is not resolved, alternative solutions are generated and implemented."[35]

Although POP and COP philosophies were develop separately over the same period of time, implementing COP requires the implementation of POP. "The goal… is for police and community to work together in solving those particular problems that cannot be solved by traditional police work and need special attention for their resolution, by developing a tailor-made response for the particular problem and situation."[36]

Police departments are just one of many agencies who share the responsibility to improve the quality of life in the community. Police officers team up with the community in a broad problem solving perspective. The Chief of Police keeps organizational values ever present in officers' minds, is an advocate for the community, and sets the tone for the delivery of law enforcement services as well as the multiagency response to quality of live issues regardless of their criminal or lack of criminal nature.

Communities across the United States have implemented COP in different ways and it has been largely successful. Different communities have different concerns and levels of interest. "Community Policing…has been one of the most effective means of diminishing the impact of gangs on neighborhoods. Community policing programs can be found at every level of government…It is also a far more effective means of policing, it requires fewer police, provides a wealth of intelligence, and capitalizes on citizen's ideas for problem solving."[37] In 2002 the Police Executive Research Foundation (PERF) conducted a survey. The results showed that, "In the area of reducing citizen's fear of crime, slightly fewer than 90 percent of the agencies replied that COP had that effect in the community in 1992, with about 95 percent in 1997 and about 98 percent in 1998."[38]

---

[35] Willard M. Oliver, *Community-Oriented Policing*, 100.
[36] Ibid.
[37] Gary D. Calese, *Law Enforcement Methods for Counterinsurgency Operations*, 43.
[38] Jason H. Beers, *Community Oriented Policing and Counterinsurgency*, 23.

International Experiences with Community-Oriented Policing

Examination of international experiences with Community Oriented Policing (COP) concentrates on three countries in different parts of the world with different cultural backgrounds. The three countries had common development of formal police forces and traditional concepts of policing. India, Nigeria, and Israel, were all former British colonies/mandates. All three countries had a cultural tradition of self policing and their British formal police forces moved away from their cultural traditions. All three of the countries faced increasing crime rates that required police to look for new and more effective social control and crime prevention strategies. The adoption of the COP philosophy helped the police and communities to develop effective mechanisms consistent with their cultural traditions.

India

In pre-colonial India, the responsibility for social control and crime prevention was provided by the village leader. The village leader appointed watchmen that assisted him by identifying strangers and suspicious people, especially at night. The British East India Company ruled India from 1600 to 1861. The company took policing responsibilities away from the village leaders and landholders. The decision conflicted with the basic traditions of village policing. It caused a chaotic situation and an increase in the crime rate. In 1903, the British appointed a committee to look into the problem. The India Police Commission restored the traditional village policing system because it was more compatible with the rural culture that called for public cooperation in policing activities. When Indian gained independence in 1947, the Constitution of India placed responsibility of policing on the state. Police were organized at the national level. The National Police Commission (1977) introduced preventive patrolling while maintaining most of the 1903 recommendations. High crime rates in the mid 1990s prompted the government to look for better crime prevention tools.

COP in India meant a shift back to their cultural traditions of policing. In 1985, police introduced the concept of special police officers (SPO). SPO were adult volunteers with no criminal record that performed tasks such as patrolling, working in rehabilitation camps, providing self defense training for young girls, and assisting victims of property crimes. They also formed committees in several specific neighborhoods, so the communities could organize neighborhood watch groups and address crime prevention issues.

An example of COP in India was the case of the community of Bhimondi in Maharashtra. This particular community had religious strife between its Hindu and Muslim residents. Police encouraged the formation of several community organizations called "Mohalla Comities"[39]. The function of these committees was to identify and solve problems in their communities. The police met with each committee on a weekly basis and agreed to help with all problems, even those that were non-criminal in nature, such as problems with electric service and food rationing. The ties between the police and the community became strong, and they were able to control the religious strife.

The India Police successfully implemented COP in spite of several challenges. There was no tradition of citizen-police interaction at a level of mutual confidence. There was a lack of formal crime prevention studies in the country. There was a lack of a criminal database arranging information in a scientific manner to support formal studies. Police being organized at the national level, local mayors had no say on police activities and operated in isolation. COP bridged these gaps.

Nigeria

Pre-colonial Nigeria had several social control and crime prevention structures. In the Northern Muslim territories, it was divided into Emirates under an Emir. Western Nigeria was organized into Oba Kingdoms each under an Obas. Eastern Nigeria was organized around

---

[39] R. K. Raghavan, and A.Sankar, Shiva, "A Communty Policing Approach to Crime Prevention: The Case of India." In *International Perspectives on Community Policing and Crime Prevention*, by Steven P. and Das, Dilip K. Lap, 113 to126. Upper Saddler River: Prentice Hall, 2003,121.

independent communities with no chief. Personal security was the responsibility of the head of each family. Each residence was built with a surrounding wall for protection. Approaches to a residence were covered with passive security measures such as barriers or guard dogs. Night time security of the property depended on the presence of the head of household. Each family head would take steps to make his presence known to any potential burglar. Each village had a village council that established a rotational community guard that would monitor the village avenues of approach to stop anyone from entering the village at night. The village councils served as the highest court for the particular village. Those territories that were part of an Emirate were under the jurisdiction of the Emir's court, and the Oba kingdoms were under the jurisdiction of their particular Obas' court.

The British colonized Nigeria as part of Lagos in 1849 and established the Lagos Constabulary to control and prevent crime at the colonial trading posts, residences, and urban centers. In 1861, the British government chartered the Royal Niger Company which established a paramilitary force to "secure colonial territory, to prevent crime, and to keep any resistance from various Kingdoms, Emirates, and towns under control."[40] That force was stationed only in urban areas and seaports. The British government took direct control of Nigeria in 1900 and established a modern police force. Police were organized at the national level and assigned to provincial and district headquarters under the provincial and district colonial officers. Crime prevention focused on the security of life and property of the colonial masters. The traditional policing mechanism remained in effect for the rest of the country.

After achieving independence in 1960, the Nigerians increased the number of officers in the police force and further divided the colonial districts to bring the police closer to the rural towns and villages. Nigerian police adopted a static law enforcement strategy. Officers did not patrol neighborhoods instead they stayed at the police station waiting for victims to report crime.

---

[40] Obe N. I. Ebbe, "Crime Prevention in Nigeria." In *International Pespective on Community Policing and Crime Prevention*, by Steven P. Lab and Dilip K. Das. New Jersey: Prentice Hall, 2003, 145.

In 1996, the government established a paramilitary unit in the Nigerian Police force to patrol "highways, busy seaports, and large city neighborhoods notorious for harboring dangerous criminals."[41]

Each local government area (LGA), comparable to a county in the United States, has a police headquarters. Each LGA uses the police to prevent crime. Villages and towns still continue to use traditional social control and crime prevention methods. Towns and villages in Southern Nigeria established associations for young adults. These organizations target individuals between the ages of 18-35 years old. The organizations prohibit their members from engaging in criminal activity. The organizations expel anyone involved in criminal behavior. Private businesses adopted passive deterrence measures and employ private security companies.

Crime prevention in Nigeria can be divided into three parts. The first is comprised of "social organizations, environmental design of the homes, neighborhood watch units, punishment for general deterrence, private security, and public education."[42] The second concentrates on identifying strangers and known burglars in the LGA and villages, and conducting community policing. The last part uses expulsion or public ridicule. "Nigerians, like people of most other African nations, believe that the best place to treat a criminal offender is in the community, not prison."[43] COP principles were compatible with their cultural traditions.

Despite political turmoil, Nigerians returned to popular participation to rebalance responsibility for crime prevention between the government and the community. Semi-authoritarian military regimes interrupted Nigeria's democratic experience. The military further intervened in the political process with the support of the population. Yet popular participation persisted through the regimes with "rhetorical acceptance of liberal democracy, the existence of some formal democratic institutions, and respect for a limited sphere of civil and political

---

[41] Obe N. I. Ebbe, "Crime Prevention in Negeria.", 147.
[42] Ibid, 149.
[43] Ibid, 150.

liberties…"[44] The military regimes accepted constitutional guarantees to return to democracy within a certain period of time. Political activity and community involvement continued within the semi-authoritarian construct. Sani Abacha's regime in the 1990s differed from the rest in that it was a totalitarian regime. In a totalitarian regime the "goal is to control completely all aspects of the political, economic and social life of its citizens."[45] Abacha used violence to repress political activity, control the media, and punish all dissent. In the end he was unable to crush all opposition political activity. Upon his death, the military established a transitional authority to return power to a democratically elected civilian government.

Israel

Israel was a former British mandate in which a patriarchal system governed the tradition of social control and crime prevention. The family elders were responsible for the conduct of all family members. Since gaining independence, the country has experienced a level of immigration that has produced a very diverse population. The diversity became a source of tension, weakened the patriarchal system, and caused adjustment problems among the youth – often expressed through criminal activity. The situation required an increase in police services. Police and the community experienced a sense of helplessness as the population became increasingly fearful of crime.

Israel is a very small country with a land mass of 7,992 square miles and faces an imminent existential threat. It is at peace with Egypt and Jordan but at war with Syria and Lebanon. The Israeli Defense Forces (IDF) has faced continuous fighting with Hezbollah in Southern Lebanon. Israel has faced many challenges including "…the struggle for economic

---

[44] Marina Ottaway. *Democracy Challenged: The Rise of Semi-Authoritarianism,* Washington, D.C.: Carnegie Endowment for International Peace 2003, 3.

[45] Bard E. O'Neill, *Insurgency and Terrorism*, 17.

24

independence, the constant threat and outbreak of war, terrorist activities, and concerns for the country's continued existence and the security of its population."[46]

The Israel Police are organized at the national level. Its funding comes from the national budget. Its mission statements include to "prevent crime, and to provide safety and security to the public it serves, working to improve the quality of life of the community."[47] The department is organized into district headquarters, sub-district headquarters, and stations. The Israel Police are also responsible for border security. It was initially, and until the late 1970s, a reactive organization that executed investigative and patrol functions. The police and the public felt that they needed more effective crime prevention methods.

Police and the Israeli community maintained close ties throughout its history through volunteer organizations such as the Community Civil Guard (CCG). Police in Israel have been able to leverage the use of the CCG in their efforts to shift toward COP. In the 1980s, they experimented with several programs. A program in Jerusalem "targeted property crimes, especially burglaries."[48] They used the CCG to disseminate crime prevention information and help people mark their property. The initiative reduced the crime rate by approximately 35 percent.[49] Another initiative established the neighborhood police officer. These officers were assigned to neighborhoods that did not have a police station and provided police services, crime prevention information to the public, and easily transitioned to the COP concept. As a result, the neighborhoods involved experienced an increased sense of security.

The Israel Police were able to implement changes in their organizational culture that made it possible to adopt COP. The Crime Prevention Units (CPU), which worked with public and private organization to standardize physical security equipment and mechanisms, became the

---

[46] Ruth.Geva, "Crime Prevention: The Community Policing Approach in Israel." In *International Perspective on Community Policing and Crime Prevention*, by Steven P. Lab and Dilip K. Das, 95-112. New Jersey: Prentice Hall, 2003, 96.
  [47] Ibid, 97.
  [48] Ibid, 100.
  [49] Ibid.

cornerstone of Israel Police COP. Police used its CPUs to introduce COP at the city level. The CPU trained officers at the stations and acted as a link with various community organizations partnering in a problem-oriented policing approach to prioritize concerns and set goals. It worked so well that many communities were able to move to further stages of the process. "The communities decided which plans should be continued, which should be retuned, and which new problems should be tackled."[50]

Analysis

After examining the experiences of non Western countries in different parts of the world, the author established a model to compare the experiences of India, Nigeria, and Israel (See Figure 1). The three countries had similar social control and crime prevention traditions. They all were former British colonies/mandates. The British established a constabulary system that each country maintained after independence. All three countries had a pluralistic political system at the time of independence. Those systems defined the population's level of participation in the political community. Semi-authoritarian military governments interrupted the Nigerian pluralistic experience but did not destroy political activity outside of the government. They maintained a long term view of returning to pluralism. Over time, the popular participation in the political communities of India, Nigeria, and Israel allowed them to adopt COP to balance the responsibility of the government and the community over social control and crime prevention.

---

[50] Ruth.Geva, "Crime Prevention: The Community Policing Approach in Israel, 105.

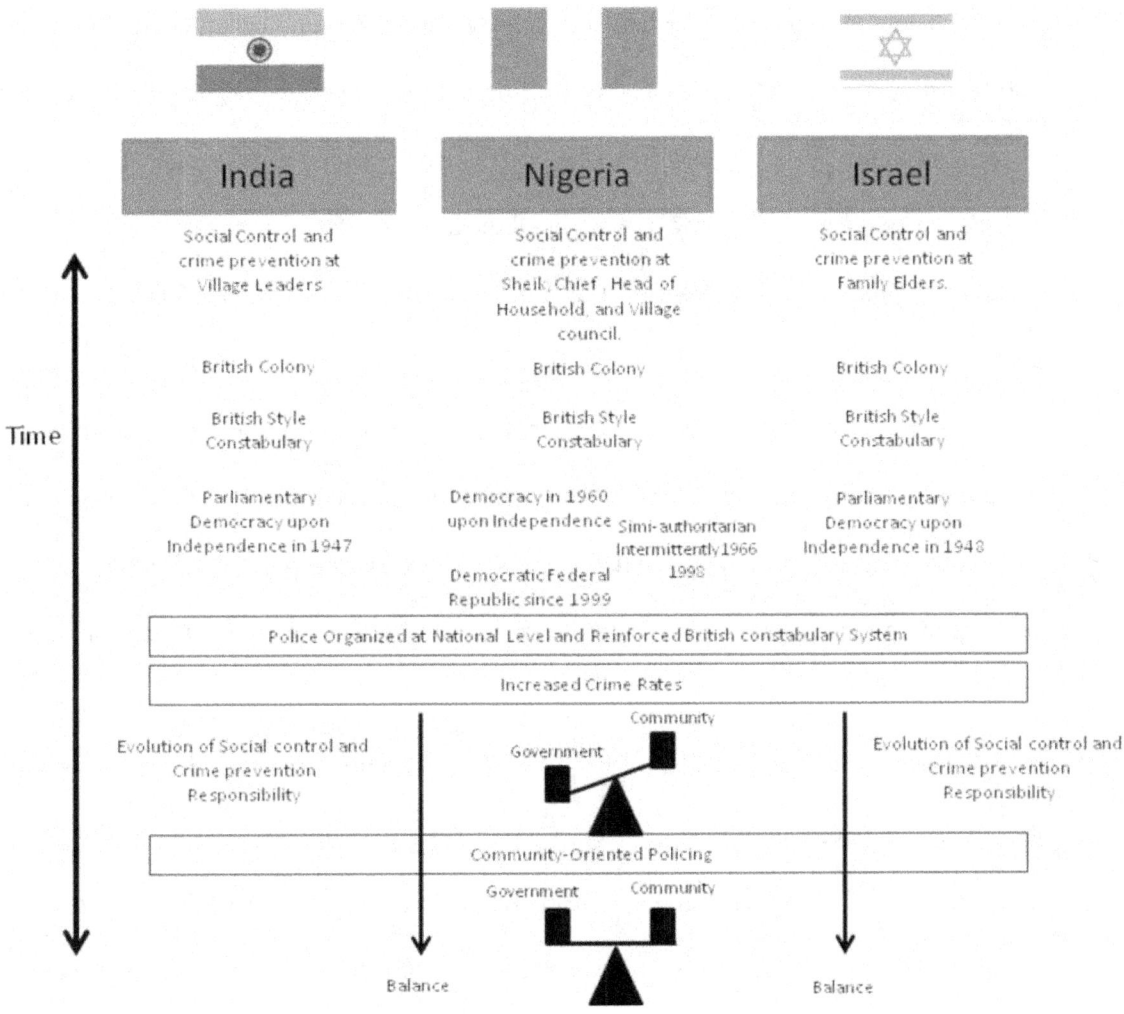

Figure 1

All three countries had social control and crime prevention traditions based on family and tribes. Indian cultural tradition placed the crime prevention responsibilities on the village chiefs. Nigeria had three different systems. In the Muslim North Islam played an important role and the tribal sheik was responsible for order maintenance. In the west, the responsibility rested on the Obas of each Oba Kingdom. The Obas was the chief. In the south, crime prevention rested on the head of household. Collective security was arranged at the village level. They had village councils but no chief. Israel had a patriarchal system in which crime prevention was the responsibility of the family elders.

All three countries were British colonies/mandates. India became a British colony in 1600 when Queen Elizabeth I placed its territory under the control of the East India Company. Nigeria became a British colony in 1849. The British crown established the Royal Niger Company in1861 to manage the new colonial territory. In 1922 Israel came under control of the British through a League of Nations Mandate when they dismantled the Turkish-Ottoman Empire.

All three countries established their police force according to the British constabulary system. The British authorities organized police at the national level with the mission to protect the colonial life and property as well as population centers and ports. In all three cases, centralizing police and crime prevention responsibilities clashed with the cultural traditions of the people and caused friction.

All three countries had a pluralistic political system at the time they became independent. India became independent in 1947 under a parliamentary democracy. Nigeria became independent in 1960 under a Governor-General this was replaced in 1963 by a democratic federal republic with a president as head of state and head of government. Israel became independent in 1948 under a parliamentary democracy.

Nigeria had several changes in its type of government though out its history. Nigeria experienced democracy from 1960 to 1966 followed by several military coups. The military maintained power until 1979 when Nigeria returned to a democratic civilian government. Public outcry over the results of the 1983 elections led to military coups in 1984 and 1985. The Nigerian Constitution of 1990 mandated the return to democracy through elections in 1992. The military government annulled the 1992 and 1993 elections. The Nigerian people revolted and public unrest led to the military government transferring power to a civilian. In 1993, a coup brought back a military government. Sani Abacha's regime was repressive.[51] While promising to return to

---

[51] Motherland Nigeria. *Historical Government.* June 13, 1998. http://www.motherlandnigeria.com/govt_history.html (accessed February 10, 2009).

return the government to civilian rule within two years he set out to eliminate all political activity. He abolished the constitution and political institutions. Popular political opposition activism continued in spite of the repressive measures. In 1998, Abacha died and the military established a transitional government. Nigeria returned to democracy through elections in 1999.

All three countries reinforced the established British constabulary system. India kept in place most of the provisions of the India Police Commission (1903). The constitution placed all policing responsibilities on the state. Nigeria kept the police organized at the national level and it strengthened its personnel to reach rural areas. Police in Israel remained organized at the national level. In all cases, police were a reactive force. The police remained at the police station and waited for citizens to report a crime.

Time and the population's level of participation in the political community were factors in balancing the responsibility for crime prevention between the state and the community in India, Nigeria, and Israel. These pluralistic systems allowed, for their populations' a high level of participation in their political communities. Over time each country's police force faced problems they were not able to solve alone. Traditional social control and crime prevention mechanisms filled the gap.

India, Nigeria, Israel are three similar cases, because they had political community that allowed for popular participation, and an established constabulary focused on social control and crime prevention. They also had police forces that placed services to the people as their premise and were willing to look for more effective crime prevention methods.

With police forces organized at the national level the responsibility for crime prevention rested on mainly on the state. All three countries experienced increase in crime rates. The search for more effective policing methods caused an evolution in the responsibility for social control and crime prevention. All three countries found in COP a means to rebalance social control and crime prevention responsibilities between the state and community.

Iraq

The Iraqi people have a rich history. Historians considered the land between the Tigris and Euphrates Rivers as the "cradle of civilization."[52] Its geographical location along main trade routes lent itself to Mesopotamians, Akkadians, Babylonians, Assyrians, Persians, Arabs, and Turks. Ancient Babylon is the source of the first known written law. Iraqis are very proud that Hammurabi's Code was the first written legal code.[53]

In Iraq, there is tension among those who prefer an autocracy, those who prefer democracy, and those who prefer a theocracy. In 1921, upon the dissolution of the Turkish-Ottoman Empire, a League of Nations mandate established the country of Iraq under the administration of the United Kingdom.[54] Iraq remained under British administration until assuming full sovereignty in 1932 as a constitutional monarchy.[55] King Faisal, and latter the Western-educated King Faisal II, had pro-Western views and worked to modernize Iraq based on their British experience. The government lasted until July 1958 when a group of army officers assassinated King Faisal II and placed General Abil al Karim Qasim in power.[56] Qasim's regime was a military-autocratic government with nationalistic and anti-Western ideas. General Qasim remained in power until February 1963 when members the Baath Party assassinated him placing the Baathist Party in charge.[57] General Hassann al-Bakr came to power in 1968. General Bakr appointed Saddam Hussein his head of security and then vice president. Saddam Hussein

---

[52] Joseph Braude, *The New Iraq: Rebuilding the Country for Its People, the Middle East, and the World,* New York: Basic Books, 2003, x.

[53] Ibid, 9.

[54] Jason Richie, *Iraq and The Fall of Saddam Hussein,* Mineapolis: The Oliver Press, 2003, 6.

[55] Central Intelligence Agency. "Iraq." *The World Factboo,*. December 18, 2008. http://www.cia.gov/library/publications/the-world-factbook/geos/iz.html (accessed January 19, 2009) and Iraq Ministry of Interior. *Iraq Today.* Baghdad: Government of Iraq, 1953, 23.

[56] John F. Devlin. "Baath Party: Rise and Metamorphosis." *JSTOR.* December 1991. http://www.jstor.org/stabel/2165277 (accessed January 15, 2009), 1401.

[57] Jason Richie *Iraq and the Fall of Saddam Hussein*, 13.

marginalized Bakr and assumed absolute power in 1979.[58] Hussein established a repressive

regime that lasted until Operation IRAQI FREEDOM in 2003. Iraq recovered its sovereignty

from the Coalition Provisional Authority (CPA) on 28 June 2004 under a parliamentary

democracy. [59] The Iraqi Constitution recognizes the supremacy of Islamic law and there are some

orthodox Islamic elements within the government that would prefer an Islamic state.

Islam is the common thread that acts as a unifying agent in the Iraqi Culture. "Islam is

perceived as providing a common identity for people of many nations."[60] The 28 million

inhabitants are 80% Arab, 15% Kurd, and 5% Turkomen and Assyrians; 97% of the population is

Muslim with the remaining 3% Christian.[61] In the cultural development of the Muslim world,

"Religion was not one aspect of life, but the hub from which all else radiated. All custom and

tradition was religious, and religious do's and don'ts extend throughout all activity, thought, and

feeling. Religion was-and for the traditional majority in all [predominantly] Arab countries has

remained-the central normative force in life."[62]

Iraqi communities are primarily Sunni Arab tribes, Shia Arab tribes, or the Kurd. Iraqi

social control and crime prevention cultural traditions are local in nature. In Arab culture loyalty

is to immediate family, extended family, the clan, sub-tribe, and tribe. The local tribal leaders and

councils are responsible for maintaining order. "The tribe provides its members with an identity, a

sense of security, and a blueprint for the resolution of conflicts."[63] Saddam Hussein's repressive

regime solidified the ties between the Arab tribes. This was especially true within the Sunni Arab

tribes. The Shia Arab tribal leaders shared some authority with the Shia religious leaders. Saddam

---

[58] Jason Richie. *Iraq and The Fall of Saddam Hussein*, 6.
[59] Central Intelligence Agency. "Iraq." *The World Factbook,* Independece.
[60] William D. Wunderle, *Through the Lens of Cultural Awareness: A primer for U.S. Armed Forces Deploying to Arab and Middle Eastern Countries*, Fort Leavenworth: Combat Studies Institute Press, 2006, 27.
[61] Central Intelligence Agency, Iraqi Population breakdown.
[62] Raphael Patail. *The Arab Mind.* New York: Hatherleigh Press, 2007,153.
[63] William D. Wunderle, *Through the Lens of Cultural Awareness,* 33.

Hussein systematically assassinated most of their religious leaders. "As a result the Shia religious establishment has been greatly weakened."[64]

The Kurds have a well established tradition of autonomy. The British promised the Kurds their own independent country at the end of World War I, but the issue remained unresolved in 1932 when Iraq gained its independence. They attempted to establish their own independent state in 1946 with the creation of the Kurdish Democratic Party of Iraq. The Kurds integrated into the political system and in 1953 changed the name of their party to the Democratic Party of Iraq "to emphasize the inclusion of the non-Kurdish communities of Iraqi Kurdistan."[65] In 1958, Qasim repressed the Kurds to consolidate his own power. When the Baath Party came to power, it initiated an Arabization campaign that destroyed many Kurdish villages. In 1970, the Kurds established an agreement with the Iraqi central government that gave them an autonomous status. Saddam Hussein embarked on a genocide campaign against the Kurds. He conducted major operations against the Kurds in 1988 and 1991. After the Gulf War in 1991, the Iraqi Kurdish region came under the protection of the United Nations and the Kurds lived under a democratic self-governing autonomous system. The Kurdish position after the 2003 Coalition invasion, was to be part of "a unified and democratic Iraq within which Kurdistan represents one of the federal political units."[66]

The Iraqi Police (IP) were organized at the national level under the Ministry of Interior- the British constabulary model. According to Arab culture, police are civil servants and are expected to serve the people. Documentation of political, economic, and social programs during the period of the constitutional monarchy suggests that this was the operational premise of the Iraqi Police. Starting in 1958, the police become an instrument of repression of an autocratic

---

[64] William D. Wunderle. *Through the Lens of Cultural Awareness*, 47.

[65] Carole A. O'Leary, "The Kurds of Iraq: Recent History, Future Prospects." *Middle East Review of International Affairs Journal.* December 2002. http://meria.idc.ac.il/journal/2002/issue4/jv6n4a5.html (accessed January 19, 2009), Timeline.

[66] Ibid, The Role of Turkey.

32

government. "even more than the military, the Iraqi police during the Saddam Hussein era were perceived to be corrupt and brutal implementers of oppression."[67]

The Iraqi police transformed from an organization that served the people to one that served the regime. Two-and-a-half generations under an autocratic form of government and Saddam Hussein's regime corrupted the Iraqi Police as an institution. The regime survived through the coercive power of several security organizations over all aspects of society as well as the Armed Forces and the Baathist Party. "In many ways, the rise of Saddam Hussein's dictatorship can be understood in terms of ascendancy of the secret police over the party and the army."[68] The Baath Party reorganized the Iraqi Police in the 1970s converting it into a para-military organization. In 1979, with the rise of Saddam, the police responsibilities included not only to enforce the law, but also to "crush political dissent and religious activism."[69] The regime did not depend on the Iraqi Police as the principal force to stay in power so it did not train or fund it adequately leading to poor public opinion for the organization and police officers becoming self serving. They supplemented their income through bribes and corruption. "Because they were not essential to the regime's survival, the Iraqi Police Services were typically under-resourced and its personnel were poorly paid, with the average policeman making around five dollars or less per month. Because of the poor pay and resources, police were not highly regarded and often supplemented their income through corruption."[70] Iraqi police were reactive and they did not patrol the streets. Like the countries examined in the previous chapter police officers waited at the police station for citizens to come in to report a crime. Even then, they reserved the right to deny

---

[67] Anthony H. Cordesman, *Iraqi Security Forces: A Strategy for Success,* Washington D.C.: Center for Strategic International Studies, 2005, 19, quote from the Department of Defense Inspertor General report on the Iraqi Police.

[68] J. Abdullah, *Dictatorship, Imperialism and Chaos: Iraq since 198,.* New York: Zed Books, 2006 Thabit A., 32.

[69] Mark R. Depue, P*atrolling Baghdad: A Military Police Company and the War in Iraq*, Lawrence: University of Kansas Press, 2007, 62.

[70] Tony Pfaff. *Development and Reform of the Iraqi Police Forces*, 7.

a citizen's call for service. An International Police Liaison Officer (IPLO) received this response in 2004 when asking about police response procedures:

> If there was any problem, a citizen would come to the station, let them know about it, and the duty sergeant would decide if it warranted their attention. If it did, he would send a policeman out. Given the hypothetical situation of immediate danger-a blaze of gunfire half a block away- the chief said the sound would be ignored unless a citizen came and insisted on intervention. Even then, we were told, it might not be considered important enough to warrant an officer's presence. The chief shrugged his shoulders. "Residents," he said through our interpreter, "they get overly concerned at the sound of gunfire in their neighborhood."[71]

The relationship between the police and the community could be different. In mid-June 2003, a Military Police platoon leader tackled the mission of re-opening an Iraqi Police station in Al Mesbah, a community in the Karradah Peninsula of Baghdad. The lieutenant did not have much luck in finding answers to his questions about the neighborhood from the station commander. He decided to go door to door and speak directly with people in the community. He explained to them that he was there to open the police station in order to provide security and prevent crime in the community. The people responded to this approach which produced an enormous amount of cooperation and good will. "With the neighborhood's cooperation and support, Al Mesbah became more secure."[72]

Several Military Police officers that served in Iraq in from 2006 through 2008 stated the challenge has been to get the Iraqi Police to develop the administrative and logistical capacity to sustain law and order operations on their own.

Iraqi Police Training

Coalition forces re-established the IP in June 2003. The initial step was to bring existing officers back to work. Many officers returned to work, but it was evident that their level of competence was low. To provide leadership, Coalition Forces to put Iraqi Army (IA) officers in charge of the IP. United States Army Military Police (MP) units train and mentor Iraqi Police.

---

[71] Robert Cole and Jan Hogan, *Under the Gun in Iraq: My Year Training the Iraqi Police,* Amherst: Prometheus Books, 2007, 106.

[72] Depue, Mark P, *Patrolling Baghdad:*, 70.

The objective is to develop their capacity to take the lead in maintaining domestic security and the rule of law. The United States Government contracted civilian police trainers to help in this transition. Iraqi police training has maintained a focus on Iraqi cultural traditions.

The author had the opportunity to observe MP units conducting the Police Transition Team (PTT) mission in Baghdad from November 2006 to May 2007.[73] The battalion responsible for Western Baghdad had a PTT assigned to the IP District Headquarters and the battalion commander had direct interaction with the IP Directorate Commander. The battalion divided the stations among its various MP Companies, and each company assigned a squad to each of the IP stations in its area of responsibility. The PTTs worked with International Police Liaison Officers to train IPs at their respective stations. IPLOs were retired and serving civilian police officers from across the United States.

The PTTs, along with their IPLO counterparts, were responsible for training and mentoring the IPs at their stations. As a whole, the MP Battalion was responsible for ensuring that the IP in Western Baghdad were proficient on all operational, administrative, and logistic functions necessary for a police department to operate. They helped the IP establish security measures, develop processes to collect criminal intelligence, and conduct their own training. Assistance to the IP ranged from helping with recruiting drives to the integration of new police academy graduates and in-service training. The objective was to bring each IP station to a level of competency in which they could plan and execute law and order operations as well as counter-insurgency operations on their own or with minimal assistance from coalition forces. The evaluation process to determine their level of readiness was based on a document called the Police Station Monthly Report (PSMR). The PSMR concentrated on the administrative, logistical, and basic police skills required when conducting law and order operations.

---

[73] Major Florentino Santana served as the Executive Officer for the 92nd Military Police Battalion from April 2006 to April 2007. He also served as a civilian Police Officer for the Metropolitan Nashville Police Department from January 1993 to July 2005. He served in the capacities of a Field Training Officer, Detective, and SWAT team Police Marksman.

Training Challenges

The IP are organized as a military organization instead of a civilian police force. The assignment of IA officers in leadership positions reinforced this problem. MP trainers reinforced military style over civilian style policing. When the army trains a police force, police look like soldiers. Use of the IPs in the COIN role became that of light infantry in a minor supporting effort to a coalition force operation. They are civilian police and should be the focus of military support in a COIN fight.

Police training was not synchronized with the training and development of the rest of the criminal justice system. The author argued during his time in Baghdad that police operational, administrative, and investigative procedures have a legal basis and must be tied to Iraqi law. This is even more important in Iraq, where a Napoleonic code justice system requires close coordination between an investigative judge and the police. There was a weak understanding of Iraqi law. Consequently, training and procedures were based on a U. S. common law framework. The United States Justice Department was the agency helping the Iraqis to re-establish their justice system, but were not operating in conjunction with police development.

There is a disconnect between what MPs call community policing and the theory behind the concept. Military Police in Baghdad complained that the IP did not know or want to engage the population and would not protect the people regardless of religious sect. The IPs remained reactive and they expected the citizens to come to them. They did not actively patrol the streets which MPs referred to active patrolling as community policing. In fact, active patrolling is just part of traditional police procedure. Recent conversations with police training personnel reveal that implementation of COP into Iraqi police training, as a logical line of operation, was eliminated from Multi-National Corps-Iraq's final plan.[74] Communication with the provost marshal section at MNC-I indicates that the multinational divisions (MNDs) do not incorporate COP in their IP training. It is the consensus that "IPs are not adequately trained nor the security

---

[74] All interviews were confidential; the names of interviewees are withheld by mutual agreement, Fort Leavenworth, KS, 26 February 2009.

environment adequate for the implementation of a program that will be effective in the long term."[75]

COP implementation will be a challenge because it is a philosophy not a program. It is a way of thinking, where police look the community's problems and figure out ways to solve them. In Iraq this could bring the police *Wasta* with the community they serve.[76]

Analysis

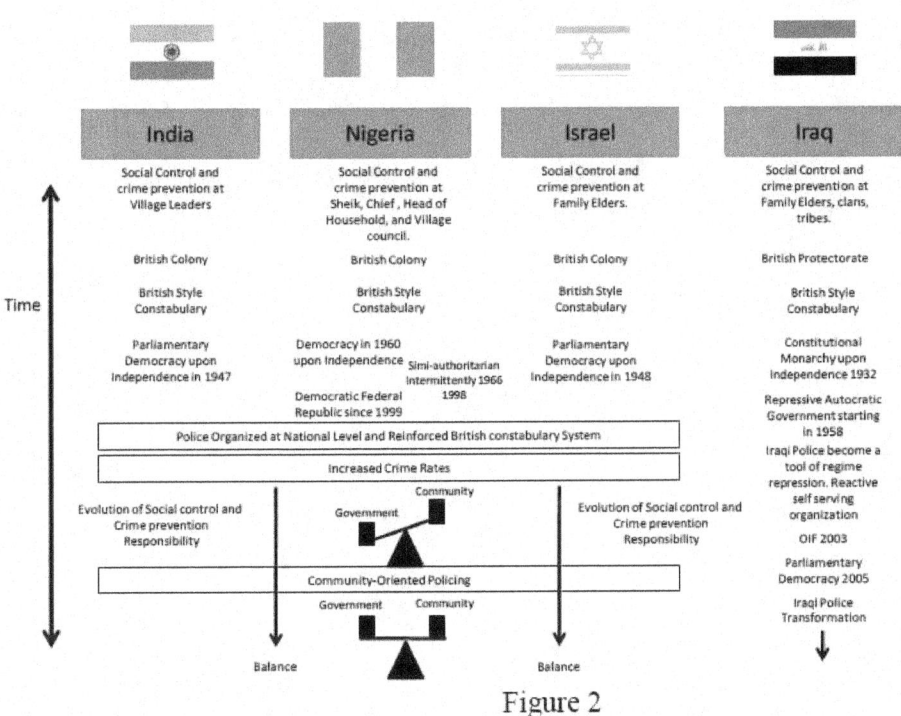

Figure 2

Evolution over time and the participation of the population in the political community were common factors that made Iraq different when compared to India, Nigeria and Israel. The countries were very similar in other aspects (See Figure 2). Saddam Hussein effectively destroyed all popular participation in the political community. The Iraqi people have no institutional memory of participation in the political community. The Iraqi Police do not have a model of what should be their relationship to the community.

---

[75] All interviews were confidential; the names of interviewees are withheld by mutual agreement, Fort Leavenworth, KS, 4 February 2009.

[76] Wasta is a term Iraqi's use when they refer to influence. An individual that has wasta within a constituency has influence.

The Iraqi Police must take the initiative in establishing a partnership with the community. Decades of living under totalitarian rule have affected Iraqi culture. Survival under the Saddam regime led people to have little trust in the government or its institutions. Under those circumstances, society defaulted to its tribal traditions for support. The Iraqi people have become used to looking at clan and tribal authority figures for direction and to fulfill their basic needs. They will not self organize.[77]

Iraqi Police training efforts could concurrently introduce a way of thinking that is compatible with the cultural traditions of the Iraqi people. Iraqi deference for authority could make it easier to implement COP from the MOI level. This is a critical period in the Iraqi Police transformation from an institution that served the state to one that serves the people and it would be most beneficial to get it right.

---

[77] William D. Wunderle, *Through the Lens of Cultural Awaremess*, 49.

Conclusion

There is much more to establishing a civilian police department than just training new officer for a few weeks on basic skills, handing them a rifles, and placing them to guard a checkpoint. International experience with law enforcement concepts is compatible with Iraqi culture. It also takes the development of a civilian bureaucracy that runs the administrative and logistical function of the department. Those are the "non-sworn" personnel that run the human resources, payroll, budget, fleet management, fleet maintenance, psychological services, and police communications. These civilians are also part of the community. When the military is placed in charge of establishing a police force it turns out looking like an army. The concentration of the work has been at the tactical level.

Training of Iraqi Police has not been synchronized with the development of the overall criminal justice system. Almost every single police rule, procedure, process, and piece of equipment has a legal basis. The police are an important component of the overall criminal justice system and cannot be developed in isolation. The Iraqi justice system requires close coordination between the investigative judge and the police. That close cooperation could diminish the weight of confessions and decrease the incidents of civil rights violations. Less civil rights violations would tend to help with ethical aspects of policing and the Iraqi Police's view of their relationship to the community.

Training of the Iraqi Police has to be based on Iraqi law, customs, culture and traditions. Police academy training cannot be divorced from the law. All training is conducted in the context of not only criminal but also civil law. The laws also define the relationship between the police and the community.

Police are the supported element in a COIN environment. Police provide enforcement and security to their neighborhoods. They are the ones with the most contact with the population.

When they are effective the COIN fight succeeds. The army supports the police, not the other way around.

COIN doctrine tells us that police are the principal government tool, yet current operations have relegated the police to a minor role. The Army is not putting into practice its own COIN doctrine in that respect. Building a police force has priority over building an army.

COP addresses all aspects previously mentioned in police development because the defined community and police relationship leverages traditional police processes to provide effective law enforcement within the legal and cultural context of the community. COP is a model of behavior to implement the changes within the Iraqi Police institution that will help them provide effective law enforcement. Effective law enforcement will increase the legitimacy of the GOI and expedite the achievement of the United States national strategic objectives in the region.

Recommendations

COP should be one of the Iraqi Police training logical lines of operation. The Iraqi culture and social control traditions are community based (family, clan tribe), which are compatible with the COP philosophy. Iraqi culture has deference for authority. Introducing the philosophy at the level of the Ministry of Interior (MOI) could allow the Iraqis to implement it from the top down. MOI could engage local leaders who would then bring along the rest of the community. Iraqi Police, who are the arm of the government with the closest contact to the community, are also part of the community. Their ability to provide effective police services, and be the link though which the government can respond to each community's concerns, will solidify the government's legitimacy. MOI and United States military advisors have to establish the conditions for COP implementation

United States military personnel must agree on a common definition of COP. The United States Army Military Police (MP) Corps should be the proponent of the definition of COP for United States forces. The definition of COP should include the civilian literature and studies on the application of the philosophy in the United States as well as around the world. It should focus on the development of civilian police departments.

The MP Corps should reinvigorate its emphasis in law and order operations. MPs need more time on patrol (re-establish Duty Officer Tours) and Junior MP Officers as well as NCOs should intern with civilian police departments. Field Grade MP Officers should attend civilian police schools and seminars. MP and civilian police partnerships can be forged through the cooperation between garrison law and order operations and departments near and around military communities. Some Army posts could even serve as regional training facilities where MPs and civilian law enforcement can share training. This will require the MP Corps to work out Army regulatory issues to encourage such cooperation. It will also require changes in human resource processes to allow MP Soldiers, who are experts in law and order operations, to contribute to the mission more effectively. Directors of Emergency Services (DES) positions should be considered commanders. In situations where there are MP Battalions on the same post, the Law and Order Detachment can remain under the DES, and coordination between the two commanders should flow as all other lateral coordination. DES personnel can be grouped in regions and respond to one of the MP brigades for Soldier administrative control (ADCON) purposes.[78]

A way to implement internship programs would be to require company grade officers in continental United States (CONUS) assignments to spend ten to twelve weeks at a major metropolitan police department. Those serving in assignments outside the continental United States (OCONUS) can do so on temporary duty and then return to their unit. It can also be achieved while on their way to the Captain's Career Corse (CCC) or on their way back to the operational Army from the CCC. The goal would be to expose company grade MP Officers to all aspects of modern police standards and give them a holistic education regarding law enforcement duties. The internship should be considered a key developmental position to ensure its implementation throughout the MP Corps. The same thing can be done for field grade officers, but they could intern with all the federal law enforcement agencies. Law Enforcement Command College and FBI Academy attendance can be expanded for majors and lieutenant colonels.

The United States Army MP Corps should be the proponent of doctrinal development for police force development that enables MP and Special Forces (SF) to conduct Foreign Internal Defense (FID) in support of strategic national objectives. Doctrine should include coordination with other agencies and expand the use of civilian police experts not only from the United States, but from around the world.

The MP Corps should also be the proponent for pre-deployment training for any unit conducting PTT. It could expand current PTT training through mobile training teams to assist Brigade Combat Teams prior to deployment.

---

[78] See appendix A

The Department of Justice must be tied into the process of police force development. It is the primary legal research agency that most police department across the United Stated, use to improve their operations. If the United States can send lawyers to Iraq to help write their constitution and train their lawyers, it can send FBI, DEA, ATF, Border Patrol, and ICE agents to ensure the criminal justice system integrates with police operations.[79] They have to be mission focused and proactive.

Training conducted by private contractors needs to expand beyond basic police skills, and the "boots on the ground" aspects of policing. Contractors need personnel experienced in the operations of large metropolitan police departments. They need expertise to train the civilian "non sworn" personnel that form the core bureaucracy and run the administrative and logistical operations. Contractors need personnel that are compatible with the cultural requirements of the supported operation and speak the local languages.

---

[79] See appendix A

APPENDIX A

ADCON – Administrative Control

ATF – Alcohol Tobacco and Firearms

CCC – Captain's Career Course

COG – Center of Gravity

COP – Community-Oriented Policing

CPU – Crime Prevention Unit

DARE – Drug Abuse Resistance Education

DEA – Drug Enforcement Agency

DES – Director of Emergency Services

FID – Foreign Internal Defense

ICE – Immigration and Customs

IDF – Israeli Defense Force

IP – Iraqi Police

IPLO – International Police Liaison Officer

ISF – Iraqi Security Forces

LLO – Logical Lines of Operation

MCO – Major Combat Operations

MNC-I – Multinational Corps-Iraq

MND-B – Multinational Division-Baghdad

MND-C – Multinational Division-Central

MND-N - Multinational Division-North

MNF-I - Multinational Force Iraq

MNF-W – Multinational Force West

MP – Military Police

NOP- Neighborhood-Oriented Policing

OIF – Operation Iraqi Freedom

POP – Problem-Oriented Policing

PTT – Police Transition Team

SOP – Strategic-Oriented Policing

SPO – Special Police Officers

APPENDIX B

What is Community-Oriented Policing?

QUESTIONS	ANSWERS
Who are the Police?	Police are the public and the public are the police: The police officers are those who are paid to give full time attention to the duties of every citizen.
What is the relationship of the police force to other public services?	The police are one department among many responsible for improving the quality of life.
What is the role of the police?	A broad problem-solving approach.
What is the role of the individual police officer?	The officer is the leader and catalyst for change in the neighborhood to reduce fear, disorder, decay, and crime.
How is police efficiency measured?	By the absence of crime and disorder.
What are the highest priorities?	Whatever problems disturb the community
What, specifically, do police deal with?	Citizen's problems and concerns.
What determines the effectiveness of police?	Public cooperation.
What view do police take of calls for service?	Vital function and great opportunity.
What is police professionalism?	Keeping close to the community.
What kind of intelligence is most important?	Criminal intelligence (information about the activities of individuals and groups.
What is the essential nature of police accountability?	Emphasis on local accountability to community needs.
What is the role of police headquarters?	To preach organizational values.
What is the role of the chief of police?	The Chief of police is an advocate and sets the tone for the delivery of both law enforcement and social services in the jurisdiction.
What is the role of the police liaison?	To coordinate an essential channel of communication with the community.
How do police regard prosecution?	As one tool among many.

Willard M. Oliver, Community-Oriented Policing: A Systematic Approach to Policing, New Jersey: Prentice Hall, 1998.

46

BIBLIOGRAPHY

Abdullah, Thabit A. J. Dictatorship, Imperialism and Chaos: Iraq since 1989. New York: Zed Books, 2006.

Baker, James A. and Hamilton, Lee H. *The Iraq Study Group Report.* New York: Vintage Press, 2006.

Beers, Jason H. *Community Oriented Policing and Counterinsurgency: A Conceptual Model.* Fort Leavenworth: Command and General Staff College, June 15, 2006.

Bender, Bryan. "U.S. Officer Spells Out Iraq Police Training Woes." *The Boston Globe .* December 13, 2006. http:www.boston.com/news/world/articles/2006/12/13/us officer spells out iraq police training woes (accessed July 30, 2008).

Bloy, Marjie. "Sir Robert Peel (1788-1850)." *The Victorian Web: Literature, History, and Culture in the Age of Victoria.* November 11, 2002. http://www.victorianweb.org/history/pms/peel/peel10.htm (accessed December 28, 2008).

Bodansky, Yossef. *The Secret History of the Iraq War.* New York: HarperCollins Publishers, 2004.

Braude, Joseph. The New Iraq: Rebuilding the Country for Its People, the Middle East, and the World. New York: Basic Books, 2003.

Bremer, L. Paul. My Year in Iraq: Ther Struggle to Build a Future of Hope. New York: Simon and Schuster, 2006.

Broadwell, Paula. "Iraq's Doomed Police Training." *The Boston Globe.* August 30, 2005. http://www.boston.com/news/globe/editorial opinion/oped/articles/2005/08/30/iraqs doomed policetraining (accessed July 30, 2008).

Bruno, Greg. "U.S. The Role of "Sons of Iraq" in Improving Security." *Washington Post.* April 28, 2008. http://www.washingtonpost.com/wp-dyn/content/article/2008/04/28/AR20080428-1120.htm (accessed September 1, 2008).

Calese, Gary D. *Law Enforcement Methods for Counterinsurgency Operations.* Fort Leavenworth: School of Advanced Military Studies, 2005.

Central Intelligence Agency. "Iraq." *The World Factbook.* December 18, 2008. http://www.cia.gov/library/publications/the-world-factbook/geos/iz.html (accessed January 19, 2009).

Chandrasekaran, Rijiv. Imperial Life in the Emerald City: Inside the Green Zone. New York: Vintage Books, 2006.

Cole, Robert and Hogan Jan. *Under the Gun in Iraq: My Year Training the Iraqi Police.* Amherst: Prometheus Books, 2007.

Cordesman, Anthony H. *Iraqi Security Forces: A Strategy for Success.* Washington D.C.: Center for Strategic International Studies, 2005.

Day, Graham and Freeman, Christopher. "Policekeeping is the Key: Rebuilding the Internal Security Architecture of Postwar Iraq." *JSTOR.* March 2003. http://www.jstor.org//stable.3095822 (accessed January 15, 2009).

Depue, Mark R. Patrolling Baghdad: A Military Police Company and the War in Iraq. Lawrence: University of Kansas Press, 2007.

Devlin, John F. "Baath Party: Rise and Metamorphosis." *JSTOR.* December 1991. http://www.jstor.org/stabel/2165277 (accessed January 15, 2009).

Ebbe, Obe N. I. "Crime Prevention in Nigeria." In *International Pespective on Community Policing and Crime Prevention*, by Steven P. Lab and Dilip K. Das. New Jersey: Prentice Hall, 2003.

Executive Office of the President of the United States. *The National Security Strategy of the United States of America.* Washignton D.C., 2002.

Executive Officer of the President of the United States. *The National Security Strategy of the United States of America.* Washigton D.C., 2006.

Friedman, Robert R. Community Policing: Comparative Perspective and Prospects. New York: St. Martin's Press, 1992.

Galula, David. *Counterinsurgency Warfare: Theory and Practice.* St. Petersburg: Hailer Publising, 2005.

Galvani, John. "The Baathi Revolution in Iraq." *JSTOR.* September 1972. http://www.jstor.org/stable/3012223 (accessed January 15, 2009).

Geva, Ruth. "Crime Prevention: The Community Policing Approach in Israel." In *International Perspective on Community Polcing and Crime Prevention*, by Steven P. Lab and Dilip K. Das, 95-112. New Jersey: Prentice Hall, 2003.

Goldstein, Herman. "Improving Policing: A Problem Oriented Approach." In *Thinking About Policing*, by Carl Klockars and Stephen D. Mstrofski. New York: McGraw-Hill, 1991.

Headquarters Department of the Army. "Field Manual 3-24." *Counterinsurgency.* Washington D.C., December 2006.

Headquarters, Department of the Army. "Field Manual 3-0." *Operations.* Washington D.C., February 2008.

Iraq Ministry of Interior. *Iraq Today.* Baghdad: Government of Iraq, 1953.

Kuhn, Thomas. "The Structure of Scientific Revolution: A synopsis from the Original by Proffessor Frank Pajares ." *Philosopher's Web Magazine.* http://www.emory.edu/EDUCATION/mfp/kuhnsyn.html (accessed June 20, 2005).

Lab, Steven and Das, Dillip K. *International Perspectives on Community Policing and Crime Prevention.* Upper Saddler River: Prentice Hall, 2003.

MNF-W G10 Staff. "Police Transition Teams for Dummies." Ramadi: Multinatinal Force-West, 2007.

Motherland Nigeria. *Historical Government.* June 13, 1998. http://www.motherlandnigeria.com/govt_history.html (accessed February 10, 2009).

National Security Council. *The National Strategy for Victory in Iraq.* Washington D.C., 2005.

Office of the Secretary of Defense. *The National Defense Strategy.* Washington D.C., 2008.

Office of the White House Press Secretary. "President Bush Announces Major Combat Operations in Iraq Have Ended." *White House.* May 1, 2003. http://www.whitehouse.gov/news/relases/2003/20030501-15.html (accessed September 30, 2008).

—. "President's Remarks at the United Nations General Assembly." *White House.* September 12, 2002. http://www.whitehouse.gov/new/relases/2002/09/20020912-1.html (accessed September 30, 2008).

O'Leary, Carole A. "The Kurds of Iraq: Recent History, Future Prospects." *Middle East Review of International Affairs Journal.* December 2002. http://meria.idc.ac.il/journal/2002/issue4/jv6n4a5.html (accessed January 19, 2009).

Oliver, Willard M. Community-Oriented Policing: A Systematic Approach to Policing. New Jersey: Prentice Hall, 1998.

O'Neill, Bard E. Insurgency & Terrorism: From Revolution to Apocalypse 2nd ed. Dulles: Potomac Books, 2005.

Ottaway, Marina. *Democracy Challenged: The Rise of Semi-Authoritarianism.* Washington, D.C.: Carnegie Endowment for International Peace, 2003.

Patai, Raphael. *The Arab Mind.* New York: Hatherleigh Press, 2007 .

Pfaff, Tony. *Development and Reform of the Iraqi Police Forces.* Carlisle: United States Army War College, 2008.

Raghavan, R. K. and Sankar, Shiva A. "A Communty Policing Approach to Crime Prevention: The Case of India." In *International Perspectives on Community Policing and Crime*

Prevention, by Steven P. and Das, Dilip K. Lap, 113 to126. Upper Saddler River: Prentice Hall, 2003.

Richie, Jason. *Iraq and The Fall of Saddam Hussein.* Mineapolis: The Oliver Press, 2003.

Ricks, Thomas E. *Fiasco: The American Military Adventure in Iraq.* New York: Penguin Group, 2006.

Rosenau, William. Low-Cost Trigger Pullers: The Politics of Policing in the Context of State Building and Counterinsurgency. Washington D.C. : RAND National Security Research Division, 2008.

Stephenson, James. Losing the Golden Hour: An Insider's view of Iraq Reconstruction. Dulles: Potomac Books, 2007.

University of Central Missouri. *August Vollmer.* October 2008. http://www.ucmo.edu/x74744.xml (accessed October 25, 2008).

—. *O.W. Wilson.* October 2008. http://www.ucmo.edu/x74741.xml (accessed October 25, 2008).

Woodward, Bob. *Bush at War.* New York: Simon and Schuster, 2002.

—. *Plan of Attack.* New York: Simon and Schuster, 2004.

Wunderle, William D. Through the Lens of Cultural Awaremess: A Primer for U.S. Armed Forces Deploying to Arab and Middle Eastern Countries. Fort Leavenworth: Combat Studies Institute Press, 2006.